HABITS THAT DEFINE POOR MANAGERS

A Rogues Gallery

Books by Terry Joseph Busch

What the Best Managers Know and Do

Effective Corporate Decision Making: Six Steps To Success

Effective Organizational Leadership: The Essential Ingredients

An Executive Trail Guide: Thinking And Behaving For Success:

HABITS THAT DEFINE POOR MANAGERS

A ROGUES GALLERY

ISBN: 97815000763176

Dedicated to encouraging
enlightened managers and management.

Acknowledgment

I am especially grateful to my friend Carol Elliott. Her insights, personal management experience, eye for the inevitable confusing sentence and sharp editorial skills were enormously helpful in shaping this book's final content.

CONTENTS

*Hood an ass with reverend purple
so you can hide his two ambitious ears and he shall pass for
a cathedral doctor.*

Ben Johnson

INTRODUCTION

All of us who have managed have occasionally done some things, behaved in some ways, or said some things we wish we could undo. Perhaps we acted on impulse where the results suggested a little more forethought would have been the better option.

But there are certain behavioral habits frequently on display in the performance of poor managers that are in a different league altogether. These habits can and usually do have long-lasting consequences. They can undermine the respect a manager's employees, colleagues and superiors have for them and ultimately undermine their effectiveness as a manager. They are practices that are very difficult to forget or forgive.

These behavioral habits often have an underlying psychological motivation that renders their occurrence difficult to alter. These habits raise serious questions about a manager's **judgment**, a personal quality none of us want others to doubt.

I have seen and experienced the impact of each of the behaviors I will discuss. I still have some vivid memories of the harm some of these habits inflicted on those unfortunate enough to work for the managers who displayed them.

I address each of these habits in hopes of encouraging all designated authority figures to be ever mindful that other human beings end up the victims of each of them. Such disrespect for others is far from the behavior we have a right to expect from those placed in charge.

I also believe that many of these habits – like all habits – can be changed. Change begins with self-awareness and a determination to alter the behavior patterns involved. The stronger, more deep-seated these habits become the more challenging the change process. So the time to begin behavior modification is always now.

For those who wish a more in-depth understanding of the anatomy of habitual behavior and successful habit change, I recommend Charles Duhigg's *The Power of Habit: Why We Do What We Do In Life And Business*. It is a fascinating and highly insightful read.

FLAT OUT LYING

The Webster Dictionary defines a **FACT** as *the quality of being actual; something that has actual existence; a piece of information presented as having objective reality; something that hinges on evidence.* So when you say *in fact,* what you are hopefully saying is *in truth* because there is actual verifiable evidence to support what you say.

Recently our public discourse has seen the emergence of an interesting unconventional phrase -- *alternative facts* -- meant to indicate there really is such a thing and we are free to choose which set of facts we wish to accept. While indeed there is a state of affairs where the potential facts concerning something are legitimately in dispute, let's be clear: once we resolve the dispute, the facts, supported by actual evidence are the only facts. Counter or alternative facts are make-believe, false representations of reality, or if you prefer, *bull shit.*

Many politicians have always engaged in a misleading representation of the facts meant to sway voters and win elections. And who among us have not stretched the truth from time to time to further a specific aim. But these prevarications are not alternative facts. They are simply lies, exaggerations, or pure BS intended to obscure facts potentially damaging to our cause.

The rub comes when we are talking about individuals in positions of authority: office holders, executives, managers, parents, teachers, physicians, lawyers, clergy, public servants, etc. The lives and wellbeing of the rest of us often depend on authority figures to tell us the truth when we seek their input no matter how unpalatable that truth. Unless in dispute or legitimate doubt, there is but one set of facts. Proffering the notion of alternative facts more to our liking becomes downright dangerous, unethical, and immoral.

We are all free to believe in what we choose. We are not, however, psychologically or emotionally equipped to be constantly confused about what is fake and what is real. A state of existence where we are routinely offered a choice between a range of alternative facts would be profoundly disorienting, emotionally traumatic, dangerous and chaotic.

Out right lying involves creating a fiction. Specifically, the invention of facts, accomplishments, experiences, and successes that do not exist. I have seen some spectacular examples complete with the disastrous consequences that often accompany them. Aspiring political candidates and job aspirants who have claimed military service never done, academic degrees never attained, professional experience never undertaken, and awards and recognition never received. Failure to achieve their immediate desired goals almost always followed.

I am not talking about the slight hyperbole or bragging that many of us often engage in when recounting something that actually happened or telling a story. Those who get to know us tend to account for this tendency and recalibrate what they hear accordingly. In many cases, the raised eyebrow of a colleague generally suffices as a self-governing device. The point remains that the basic components of the story are true. In **conscious fabrications,** the basic components of a story are not true. They are inventions designed to let others know how impressive, important, influential, or downright talented the storyteller is.

How do we actually know that what we are hearing is a lie? In many instances we do not and will not if the fabricator is clever, a skilled yarn spinner, and disciplined enough to pick their spots and frequency carefully. The trouble is that this practice tends to become habitual and eventually transparent to those who have heard one too many tall tales.

Some managers in my experience have had difficulty keeping their stories straight, rendering them vulnerable to comparing notes. In other instances, circumstances have required verifying a fabricated account of something a manager has claimed thus revealing the actual truth. Most often this tendency to make-up things designed to impress produces through its frequency its own common-sense transparency.

Like other bad management habits, flat out lying raises basic questions about a manager's honesty and maturity. It also tends to erode the mutual trust and respect that is essential to an effective manager-employee relationship.

In the age of email, Facebook, and Twitter, we are all frequently reminded of how impossible it is to ever retract something once it enters the public domain. False claims once aired remain an ever-present danger to our reputation for honest self-disclosure regarding who we actually are and what we have actually accomplished.

What the best managers know is that their reputation for managerial excellence will ultimately be defined by the performance of those they manage, not by their image. They are content to simply manage and leave the image creating to others. They understand that it is always better to allow others to occasionally sing their praises, than to constantly and falsely blow their own horns.

Rejecting Blame

I have known my share of managers who seem determined **to pass along blame for any and all mistakes.** These are the managers who not only shirk responsibility for their own actions but who fail to understand that being a manager makes them the **Captain of the ship.** As Captain they are responsible and accountable for everything that happens beneath their authority like it or not.

For these managers there are always mitigating circumstances that allow them -- *by their own logic* -- to pass the buck. Because doing this is usually so blatantly obvious to everybody around them, it is easy to see how it impacts the respect and esteem in which these managers are held. The fact that a manager may not have known about a mistake as it was happening is irrelevant to employees who expect the boss to assume his appropriate level of accountability.

It is unpleasant when a superior calls you out for a mistake an employee has made and of which you were oblivious. But the best managers accept that as part of the job. They might even consider telling their boss: *how about I come to your office later for a flogging after I have taken the steps needed to find out what happened and fix whatever needs fixing.*

Managers who are quick to blame others for things, generate a great deal of irritation and anger among employees for what is invariably seen as a character deficiency and immaturity. Blame avoidance also has a deadening effect on creativity and risk taking because these activities inevitably lead to errors and mistakes. Knowing that the boss will seek to distance herself from anything that goes wrong, employees will generally choose not to take the chance.

Equally damaging, every manager must at times be a leader. Being a leader means occasionally asking employees to: venture into uncharted waters; try new things; adapt to changes they may not wish to embrace; and to take risks. For employees to follow such leadership, they must respect and trust that their boss is someone they can count on to accompany them in facing an uncertain future. Bosses who simply cannot help but blame others for things that go awry gradually mortgage their ability to lead.

These managers usually fail to impress the majority of their superiors who will come to see this habit of rejecting blame as a serious flaw. While this poor management practice alone may not derail a managerial career, it is rarely ignored in well- managed organizations in making important management postings.

Do not let this happen to you. No matter how painful it sometimes is to accept blame for something for which you are accountable as the boss, have the maturity to do so.

TAKING CREDIT FOR OTHER PEOPLE'S WORK

As I write about each of these behavioral habits, I find myself unable to decide which of them is more irritating, infuriating, frustrating, or just plain unacceptable from the standpoint of an employee. Suffice to say this one -- taking credit for the work of others -- is right up near the top.

As a Freshman in college, I vividly recall the number of times one of my professors made plain the definition of plagiarism and elaborated upon the many forms in which they had experienced it. The penalties at my university for plagiarism were quite severe, as was the likelihood of eventually getting caught should I be dishonest and stupid enough to give it a try. I trust most of today's managers had similar experiences at some point during their educational journey.

The core message we all received regarding taking credit for something done by someone else is it is *dishonest* and *wrong*.

In the workplace, this habit in a manager is rarely as blatant and easily detectable as trying to pass off a *Reader's Digest* article as your class term paper. This habit is more insidious because it usually happens behind the proverbial closed-door when a manager passes off as their own the accomplishment of an employee or colleague. In many cases, the innocent victim of this lie remains unaware unless by some chance accident they happen upon the truth.

I leave it to others to speculate upon a manager's motivation for engaging in this dishonest behavior. I believe it is more important to focus upon the two critical reasons why this particular trait is so harmful and potentially self-destructive.

One of a manager's most important responsibilities is the showcasing of their employee's talents, potential and accomplishments. Without their manager's willingness to give honest credit where it is due, an employee's path to career success and advancement becomes substantially and unfairly harder. Taking behind-the-back credit for what one's employee thinks and does leaves the employee in the dark and represents a betrayal of trust.

Because this behavior tends to become an habitual pattern, it almost certainly will eventually come to light. An employee, colleague or superior will at some point uncover an instance or two of misrepresenting the true author of something and call into question the manager's honesty. If this happens often enough, the damage to a manager's reputation and career can become permanent.

Once our honesty is called into doubt and backed by facts, the damage is difficult to undo. It can take a great deal of time and contrary evidence to regain the trust others will again have in what we say. Couple the potential personal damage with the harm done to those whose accomplishments and ideas were dishonestly claimed as one's own and it is easy to see why the best managers avoid doing this.

BANKRUPTING ONE'S WORD

You have my word.

Throughout written history -- Western history at least -- the phrase *you have my word* has carried significant symbolic meaning. It is often paired with the concept of **honor** and invariably communicates an important **contract** between the person who gives their word and the individual to whom that word is given.

I have occasionally known a few managers whose frame of reference for giving their word is *politics,* where it often seems that breaking one's word for a variety of reasons is perfectly alright and consequently understood as the nature of the process. I believe such thinking by a manager is dangerous and seriously undermining in the long run.

Although elected to office and therefore beholden to one's constituents in many ways, a politician's relationship with the voters is fundamentally different from that of a manager with their employees. As a manager, you generally have the power to hire and fire those entrusted to your management skills, influence their pay and bonus decisions, and create the opportunities that will help determine their professional advancement. That sort of power over specific individuals is beyond that of a typical politician.

For a manager's relationship with his employees to work effectively, a solid level of trust that goes both ways is essential. A manager asks employees to accomplish many things, any number of them tasks they would rather avoid. Implicit in an employee's willingness to comply is the word of their manager that she will support them, have their back when required, follow through on whatever promises and commitments she has made, and do everything possible to help ensure that they succeed professionally.

When a manager promises an employee something, from the employee's point of view the manager has given her word. The integrity of that verbal contract is important to the employee and breaking it has consequences. Break these contracts often enough and a manager in essence **bankrupts the value of their word**. When one's word or promises have little value, trust and loyalty and a willingness to follow a manager's lead inevitably suffer.

There are times when changing circumstances necessitate revisiting a promise or commitment that is no longer possible or prudent to fulfill. The best managers view these situations as an opportunity for a discussion aimed at explaining the reasons they believe a different course of action is now required. These conversations represent a sign of respect for the employee's ability to fairly consider -- if not like -- what they hear and make adjustments in their expectations if required. The best managers never simply renege on a promise no explanation given or seemingly required.

A wise manager thinks carefully about the promises he makes and the specifics of a circumstance where they give their word. It is better to acknowledge uncertainty, doubt, and withhold commitment when necessary than to make a promise one's gut feeling suggests they may regret. Protecting the reliability and dependability of their word is among the most valuable things a manager can do and makes their relationships with employees, colleagues, and superiors a lot easier.

It has been years but I still vividly recall the sad aftereffects of a broken management promise by one of my employee managers at the time. The manager had apparently given their word on numerous occasions to an employee that a coveted position would be theirs as soon as the current incumbent moved on. Yet when the time came to fill the position and I asked the manager for his recommendation, a different employee was his choice. I accepted his recommendation and was soon confronted by the aggrieved employee whose anger -- bordering on fury -- and sense of betrayal was barely contained. Within months the angry employee had departed, the sad tale had spread throughout the organization, and the damage to the value of the manager's word was complete.

When it comes to giving someone your word, mean it and follow through on the commitment or do not give it at all.

ABANDONING SHIP

Abandoning ship is a close relative of reject-ing blame but is sufficiently different in its dynam-ics and insidiousness to warrant a separate discussion.

Sometimes this behavior takes the form of exces-sive *procrastination* or *laziness.* In these instances man-agers abandon the responsibility for decisions and action that comes with the job, either out of fear of making mis-takes or a willingness to let their employees do various parts of their job. Over time, procrastination and laziness under-mines employee confidence that their boss is up to their job.

To illustrate another form of abandoning ship pic-ture a lively meeting between a manager and his staff. Col-lectively they have a challenging work-related problem to solve and they are discussing various alternative solutions. Two approaches emerge as having the most potential for resolving the problem. The manager finds himself in fa-vor of option one, while the staff is strongly inclined toward option two. The discussion continues for a while but it be-comes clear the two sides are to remain apart. What next?

The manager as the boss can simple say *we are going to do it my way.* He will be held accountable for the outcome and it is perfectly acceptable for him to make the call. The staff may feel a bit disgruntled but they did have their say.

However, suppose our manager at some point, throws up his hands and says something like this: *OK, I'm tired of argu-ing. Enough! Have it your way. We'll go with option two but I'm sure it isn't going to work and just remember, I told you so.*

What has just happened here? Does our staff of employees feel *empowered*? Or do they feel *abandoned*? Does our staff believe their boss will join them in making a full effort to make option two succeed? Or do they most likely suspect that he will remain on the sidelines secretly rooting for the entire effort to fail? For the sake of group cohesiveness, wouldn't it have been better for the boss to simply insist on option one rather than take the course he did, a course I refer to as *abandoning ship*.

When a manager invites her employees to join her in discussing how to address a problem, a **partnership** relationship is implied. Although she may choose a course of action that is not universally supported by the entire staff, she will in exchange for having been consulted, expect the staff to try their best to make that decision work. She will not appreciate sabotage or slow rolling.

Employees similarly expect the same total commitment from the boss, when he has given the blessing of his authority to a course of action. Luke warm, passive, indifferent, or non-existent involvement *mocks* the notion of a partnership. It is better for a manager to withhold permission entirely.

The act of a manager's abandoning ship is often quite subtle but employees intuitively know when it has occurred, when they are on their own, and when they alone will need to bear the full burden of making something succeed. If that something fails, they know that the manager will point the accusing finger squarely in their direction.

Because of the destructive nature of this passive aggressive managerial behavior on a work unit's ability to function as a team, I have always been a bit baffled by its occurrence. Since in the eye's of a manager's superiors, they will be held accountable anyway for any outcome whether they stood on the side lines or not, why not put the full weight of their influence behind achieving a success?

As a manager, it is always better to simply say *it's my call, I'll be held accountable, so we will do it my way*, than to undermine your authority and trust by seeming to acquiesce then cast your employees adrift. The best managers always put their full personal support and effort behind every decision they make or sanction.

Few employees will put up with an abandoning manager for longer than necessary. And even fewer competent senior executives will view such behavior by a junior manager as qualifying them for higher management responsibility.

As you ponder the significant consequences of abandoning ship, the following example offers a chilling reminder:

On the evening of January 13, 2012 the Italian cruise ship Costa Concordia under the command of Captain Francesco Schettino drifted off course and struck the rocks off the coast of the island of Giglio on Italy's West Coast. Despite panic among the ships 4,229 passengers and crew, evacuation procedures did not begin for almost an hour after the collision. By that time the ship was already taking on water, seriously listing to starboard, and the lifeboats on the starboard side were unusable.

Captain Schettino meanwhile had abandoned the bridge and although ordered by an Italian Port Official to return to his ship immediately, he refused to comply. The ships Second Master had also left the bridge with over 300 passengers and crew still on board. So a confused, ill-informed, disorganized and leaderless ship crew was left to evacuate frightened and panicky passengers, in the dark, on their own. That only 32 passengers died seems rather remarkable under the circumstances[1].

---

1 See WWW.brecoder.com/top-news/109-world-top-news/224088-t imelineofitaliancruiseshipdisasrer.

DEMEANING OR BULLYING OTHERS

If you have ever received a highly personal or profane verbal attack from a boss, you know how embarrassing, demoralizing, emotionally traumatic, and infuriating that can be. It's even worse if it was done in public.

Personal, demeaning, and abusive verbal attacks can undermine an individual's self-confidence and self-esteem, lower workplace morale, and crush the human spirit. No wonder so many employees search the web for advice on dealing with a verbally abusive boss. Personally abusive behavior by a manager is *never OK*.

I will leave it to the psychologists to explain why certain individuals do this to others. I will simply say that as a manager, nothing you encounter in the behavior or performance of one of your employees is sufficient to justify making your response personal or abusive.

Employees can drive a manager crazy. After all, *they are just people.* They make mistakes, repeat the same mistakes, forget things, frustrate a manager's plans and goals, fall short of their expectations, behave in inexplicable ways, and occasionally – despite a manager's best efforts -- prove unsuited for their jobs.

Because a manager is human, employee behavior will frequently elicit a predictable range of negative feelings and emotions: stress, frustration, anger, incredulity, astonishment, and perhaps even something close to rage. It can be very hard not to let such feelings out when they overwhelm us but the best managers have learned the importance of controlling the *time, place, method, and format* of their response. This is perhaps one of the most important elements of self-management that a manager must achieve.

The best **time** for delivering critical feedback to employees is always as close to the precipitating event as possible because it remains fresh in everybody's mind. When managers find themselves feeling overly emotional and upset, it should also be after they have cooled down. Then it is easier to focus on the specific behavior or event, not on the individual and how the manager feels. A simple *let's talk later* usually provides the breathing space needed to get a critical response right.

As for **place** it's simple, **never in public**. No matter what an employee has done, the humiliation and embarrassment that accompanies a public flogging is never justified. Even assuming a manager wishes others to know that certain things are unacceptable, trust me they will get that message even when the critical conversation is behind closed doors. Employees have a way of knowing when a colleague has had a talking to.

The **method** for critical feedback should always be **in person, direct,** and **verbal**. While this may seem obvious, many managers have difficulty giving direct, specific, critical feedback because they fear the uncomfortable emotions that often accompany such situations. As author Joseph Grenny points out in his bestselling book *Crucial Conversations*; issues not talked out are invariably acted out. Harsh looks, avoidance behavior, excessive micromanagement, or frequent sarcastic remarks are just as demeaning as a harsh personal attack.

The **format** for critical feedback should always **focus on the behavior or event** that necessitates the conversation. It should avoid characterizations of the individual's personality, intelligence, basic competence or value as a person, or assumed motivation and cause. What a manager knows is what they saw or have verified and the reason it is unacceptable in the workplace. It **is** a manager's job to insist that employees meet widely agreed upon standards for performance and behavior and to insist they take the necessary corrective action when required. It **is not** a manager's job to judge in any way an individual's basic value as a person.

What do you do as an employee when you feel you are being confronted in an abusive or bullying way? First, remember it's the manager who has the larger problem not you. Second, personal abuse does not solve any problem, is irrational, and is immune to argument and reason. Do not respond in kind. Finally, it is perfectly permissible for you to walk away indicating that you are prepared to listen only when they have cooled down and are willing to discuss the actual issue itself.

SETTING OTHERS UP TO FAIL

Making personnel moves is a routine part of most managers' jobs. It is also one of the most critical elements of a manager's responsibilities whether looked at from the organization's or the individual assignee's perspective. From the organization's vantage point, getting the right people in the right jobs translates into quality output and top performance. From the individual's perspective, it is about job satisfaction, motivation, morale, self-confidence, a sense of making a difference, and self-fulfillment.

In their bestselling book *First, Break All The Rules (P. 67)* authors Marcus Buckingham and Curt Coffman make a compelling case that the best managers place enormous emphasis on talent, individual strengths and on finding the right fit in making every personnel assignment. According to the authors, the best manager's are consistently guided by a simple mantra: *People don't change that much. Don't waste time trying to put in what was left out. Try to draw out what was left in. That's hard enough.*

But what happens when for whatever reason a manager manages *to place a square peg in a round hole?* This is what I call **a set up to fail** and it can have serious consequences all around.

Fans of mystery and detective stories understand the phenomena called **a set up**. The victim initially is unaware that their situation will likely result in an outcome detrimental to their well being. The ultimate discovery by the victim that they had little control over or ability to alter their fate is painful, frustrating and demoralizing. The victim generally ends up feeling manipulated, disrespected and angry. Most managers understand that this is no way to treat anybody entrusted to their management skill but it can happen by mistake, ignorance and despite the best intentions.

The odds of assigning people correctly go way up when a manager fully understands the nature of the post she is about to fill. This begins with a clear comprehension of the purpose, goals, and relevance to the organization's business or mission of the position and the skills, talents, and experiences the occupant will need to succeed. Match these two criteria carefully, provide a clear set of expectations, add in the right amount of coaching and mentoring, and successful performance is usually the result.

Even the best managers do not always get it right. Many managers get it wrong far too often for a variety of reasons:

- They pick a friend, favorite colleague, or decide to fill some quota without regard for position requirements, strengths, or skills;

- They display gender or racial blindness in compiling the assignment pool, thereby potentially overlooking some better choices;

- Or they simply do not undertake the necessary home-work needed to fully understand what the specific individuals they are considering can and can't do.

The consequences of a bad assignment decision only magnifies when a manager or management insists that the problem lies with the assignee not with the bad decision. When we humans fail at something for whatever reason, many of us place a great deal of the blame on ourselves but that does not exonerate managers from blame for their contribution to a poor assignment call.

Managers are the ones ultimately responsible for ensuring that people with the right talent, strengths, and skills are matched with the jobs under their authority. No matter how much someone may want and lobby for a particular assignment or may personally feel they have all the attributes required, the best managers will say **no** and **why** when their best judgment tells them somebody else is better suited to the task at hand,.

Bad assignment decisions always have a high potential for failure. That is why the best managers work hard to make very few of them. When they do error, they are quick to acknowledge their mistake and take corrective action in a way that both serves their organization and hopefully preserves the dignity and self-confidence of the victim of that mistake.

Enabling a Problem By Ignoring The Problem

In most of my management workshops, the discussion at some point generally comes around to one of those workplace problems that few managers are eager to confront. Beyond the obvious substandard performance discussions that will need addressing, consider the following:

- A personal hygiene issue;

- The frequent use of inappropriate language around co-workers;

- A suspected alcohol or drug abuse issue;

- A suspected violation of workplace time and attendance requirements;

- Behavior of any kind that demonstrably lies outside usual and expected organizational norms;

- An employee's anger management difficulties;

- Excessive displays of negativity and an argumentative disposition;

- Potential sexual harassment behavior;

- The proselytizing of co-workers motivated by one's political or religious beliefs.

Many managers would rather avoid confronting others regarding their poor performance or any of the above issues. Such conversations are difficult, likely to elicit emotional and defensive responses, and in some instances hurt feelings and negatively effect working relationships Some managers do avoid or skate gingerly around difficult issues to the detriment of teamwork, workplace morale, and often productivity.

It's important for managers to step back and take a clear-eyed look at what avoidance behavior actually amounts to: **by ignoring the problem, the manager is enabling, authorizing, and unconsciously encouraging its perpetuation.** Why should an employee stop doing anything if their manager isn't prepared to confront the behavior or performance involved?

An accessory after the fact in criminal law is a person who having knowledge that a crime has been committed, aids or attempts to aid the criminal to escape apprehension. These accessories are frequently prosecuted for their enabling collusion.

An accessory after the fact in management terms is a manager who knowingly and willfully ignores potentially damaging workplace problems. This avoidance behavior renders the manager equally responsible and accountable for the problem he has ignored.

There are three compelling reasons for a manager to avoid enabling problem behavior and performance through avoidance.

First, assuming the manager is a member of a larger organizational management team, she is responsible for ensuring that problems within her scope of responsibility are resolved, not passed on to other managers or parts of the organization. I know this happens all the time and is characteristic of some organizational cultures but *passing the buck* remains an abdication of a manager's responsibility and a detrimental part of any working culture.

Second, ignoring a clear problem almost always has some deleterious impact on a manager's direct working unit or team. This is often hard to see if other folks are not complaining but it is a safe bet that the negative impact is there.

Any persistent problem manifested by one individual is likely to affect his teammate's morale and overall team performance. You can bet that those most affected by the problem individual's behavior will expect the manager to do something about it. They are likely to feel angry and frustrated if their manager does not.

Third, it is unfair, callous, and disrespectful for a manager to passively enable an employee to perseverate in behavior likely to eventually result in career damage, negative personnel action, and perhaps termination of employment. All designated authorities are expected to try and protect individuals under their authority from harm. This includes sometimes protecting them from themselves. While no manager can personally fix an employee's performance or behavior, they certainly can humanely, objectively, and forcefully make clear that the employee must get whatever help necessary to address their problems.

NOTHING IS EVER GOOD ENOUGH

We all know a version of the tale where a child brings home a report card filled with As and one lone B. Beaming with pride she hands the card to a parent and receives the following response: *what happened with this B?* The really sad part of this tale is that all of us probably know someone -- perhaps ourselves -- that had this happen to them as a child and the scars still hurt.

As a management consultant, I have heard my fair share of this same tale from employees whose boss never seems to be satisfied. In a recent conversation an employee told me how proud she was about regularly exceeding a numerically measured weekly production goal. Yet in her most recent performance review, the boss did not praise but rather questioned why that goal wasn't being met on a daily basis as well. It did not seem to matter she said that she was being productive by meeting the weekly goal. Nor did the boss seem interested in trying to understand why some days were necessarily dedicated to numerous non-measured but essential work tasks.

Was this employee angry? Yes. Frustrated? Yes. Did she feel that exceeding a mandated weekly goal was simply an irrelevant, unappreciated fact? Yes. Was she thinking there might be a better place to work? Perhaps. Was she motivated to approach tomorrow's work with passion, initiative, and creativity? I doubt it.

In fairness I have no idea what this boss actually thought about the employee's performance, nor what impression they wished to convey. Perhaps he had some motivational intent. All I know is that as far as she was concerned, almost no level of performance was likely to be good enough for this boss.

Providing performance feedback is a daily element of any manager's job. Some performance-related behavior will warrant high praise and some will require constructive criticism. Regardless of the feedback's content, the parts any manager controls are **how** and against **what backdrop** the feedback is delivered.

In considering the how and the backdrop, it is wise to keep our human nature in mind. Affirmation, admiration, and praise for our accomplishments from our authority figures, loved ones, and respected others are powerful motivators and strong encouragement for repeat performances. The best managers try never to miss opportunities to recognize and affirm the accomplishments of their employees. The message the employees receive is that their performance is appreciated and valued, and that many things they do are good enough to satisfy the boss.

Consider what might have been the outcome in our example had the boss begun his performance review by praising his employee's weekly goal-surpassing efforts and status as one of the unit's highly productive individuals. He might then have broached the daily performance issue by asking what part of the unit's daily routine currently gets in the way of a goal-directed focus, perhaps suggesting a willingness to consider eliminating any unnecessary busy work. Do any of us believe the impact on this employee would have been the same?

The best managers intuitively understand the power and positive effect of recognition. They realize that generally speaking, what they see in most employee performance is pretty darn good and that often 85 % is infinitely better than the time wasted seeking absolute perfection.

Above all, good managers studiously avoid constantly emphasizing the flaws, shortcomings and missing elements in an employee's performance, while ignoring the good. They recognize the damaging consequences of being perceived as a boss for whom no effort will ever be quite good enough.

The best managers create a positive relationship with their employees based upon consistent recognition of their efforts and accomplishments. This helps build employee trust in a manager's intentions, communicates the manager's concern for and belief in the employee's ability to succeed, and suggests the manager's willingness to participate in achieving that success.

Good managers give employees possibilities to realize not rigid expectations against which their value will be judged. When performance expectations are not met, the discussion is more likely to focus on what now needs to be done by both employees and the boss, rather than on how disappointed the boss happens to be.

Against a **positive backdrop,** occasions where negative feedback and constructive criticism must be delivered are much easier for an employee to accept. We all know we aren't perfect but we simply don't want to constantly hear only about our flaws.

AVOIDING THE EMOTIONAL SIDE OF MANAGEMENT

For many years, I have heard the phrase **touchy feely** used by managers of both genders to describe a variety of things and behaviors in the workplace. *Oh, you mean that touchy feely stuff* or *I don't do that touchy feely thing*, or *this isn't going to involve that touchy feely business* are commonly what you hear. But what do expressions like this actually mean and convey about the person who frequently uses them?

It is impossible to know what attitudes lie behind the use of the touchy feely phrase by any specific individual. Yet, I can never recall hearing anybody say anything like *I truly enjoy and look forward to the touchy feely side of management.* I can only conclude that the phrase has a somewhat negative, dismissive, something to be avoided, or something for others to do connotation for most of those who use it.

The phrase is almost always used by managers to describe aspects of managing actual human beings. These aspects involve **emotion-laden** topics like:

- Personal feelings;

- Sensitivity;

- Self-disclosure;

- Human life experiences;

- Temperament;

- Relationship and trust building;

- Human shortcomings and self-destructive behavior;

- Conflict management;

- Cultural differences;

- Pain and suffering;

- Self-esteem and confidence issues;

- And the inter-personal requirements for team and community building.

When uttered by many males, I have often sensed that this phrase represents a code for activities best left for women to do. .

One reason I have never cared for the phrase is that it feels like a pejorative, patronizing insult directed at those who appear too attentive to feelings and emotions. Its use conjures up the notion of a topic its user feels far too dangerous or personally threatening to warrant much serious attention. The phrase reveals a fundamental misconception -- or deliberate act of denial -- concerning the realities of managing: **everything about managing is always about people, their emotions and all**.

What the best managers understand is that there is no distinction between the job or mission components of an organization and the people management side. They are the same thing, inextricably interconnected. It is business or mission through people and all that reality demands of those who manage. I have often asked a client or workshop participant to name one thing they do as a manager that does not have human beings attached to it in some way. I am still waiting for an answer.

The best managers understand that if they hope to be good at their job, they must regularly access the broadest possible range of their thinking, emotional, and behavioral repertoire. They reject out of hand any notion that management skills fit simplistically into a taxonomy labeled *hard* or *soft*. They absolutely reject any notion of gender specific behavior.

The best managers grasp that all of us have the potential to respond to others across a broad intellectual and emotional range. The real issue is **situational appropriateness.** I have seen extraordinary managers of both genders at work. They have exhibited exceptional decisiveness, tough-mindedness, cool-headed logic, and a purposeful assertiveness when required. They have also demonstrated exceptional insight into human nature, understanding, warmth, and compassion in building and motivating a cohesive, high-performing team.

I have also seen certain male managers lampooned for seeming too comfortable with the emotional side of their job and many female managers typecast either as softies because of their emotional expressiveness, or saddled with unflattering labels for their assertiveness and toughness. While our society has not always helped by perpetuating many of these negative gender stereotypes, the best managers manage to ignore them.

The best managers are legitimately who they are, comfortable in their own skin, not overly identified as man or woman, just simply as **me.** This creates a sense of authenticity that makes them managers with whom we wish to work. Time, I think, managers relegate the phrase touchy feely to the dustbin of history where it belongs.

SUMMARY THOUGHTS

There are quite a few professions where the consequences of mistakes, bad professional practices, or serious errors in judgment are quite easy for us to imagine. Airline
pilots, surgeons, dentists, criminal lawyers, structural en-
gineers, cruise line captains, and school bus drivers readi-
ly come to mind. Most of these professions require some
form of insurance to cover the possibility of their errors.

Unfortunately, I cannot recall a single instance during my
management career where a group of us sat down to discuss
the impact of our mistakes and occasional acts of poor judgment. This failure of many managers to ever come to grips with
the consequences of bad management for their *organizations* and
workforce is even more egregious when you consider the ubiq-
uitous global nature of poor management habits and behavior.

While it is almost impossible to realistically assess the *organizational impact* of a single poor manager, poor management practices and behavior are often widespread in many
organizations. They are perpetuated because the practices in
question have become a part of the organization's overall management culture and are frequently rewarded not punished.

Whether the byproduct of a poor selection process for managers, inadequate supervision, too little attention to management
training and best practices, or upper management's failure to
insist that the practices taught in management training courses
are concurrently demanded in daily manager behavior, the broad
impact of poor management is measurable and observable in
the characteristics of an *under-performing organization*. Any
manager, who argues that their organization functions at its
best despite bad management practices, is only fooling them-

selves. I suggest they seek a more objective observer's opinion and demand some hard evidence to support their claim.

In the best organizations management itself takes full ownership of every part of the management selection, development, training, evaluation, and assignment process to ensure consistency and harmony of philosophy and practice. In top performing organizations, management fully comprehends the essential link between good management practices and a highly motivated, creative, and productive workforce. Insisting on good management becomes almost an obsession, as does the frequent monitoring of actual manager performance and tangible results.

A negative impact on organizational performance and productivity is far from the only toll bad management habits inflict on an enterprise. The human toll is equally if not more destructive. It is a demoralizing force. Where bad management is endemic within an organization, it is a safe bet that many of the most talented and potentially productive members of a workforce will underperform and beat a hasty path toward the exit doors as soon as they can.

The *human impact* of bad management is relatively easy for most of us to understand, because so many of us have been the victims of it at some point in our careers. The symptoms we feel and experience run a wide gamut:

- Stress, anxiety, headaches, disgruntlement, frustration, and depression;

- Periods of complaining to anybody who will listen at work and often to our significant others at home;

- That churning feeling in our stomachs both on the way to and from work;

- A tendency toward distraction at work and when we are with our families, loved ones, and friends;

- Difficulty sleeping because we simply can not let go of our unhappiness at work;

- An occasional tendency to take out our frustrations inappropriately on the innocent around us.

If the above sounds like a rather horrible series of consequences to inflict on someone else, then it bears constant reminding that managerial mistakes, errors in judgment, and poor professional behavior carry a potentially serious, negative human impact. I believe the more frequently any professional reminds themselves of the potential damage they can do both to their organization and the individuals for whom they are responsible, the more likely they are to dedicate themselves to being the very best possible doctor, lawyer, pilot, school bus driver, structural engineer, cruise ship captain, and yes manager.

The best managers:

Never believe they are good enough;

Never assume they always get it right;

Never think they have all the answers;

Never lose sight of the fact that their next mistake may lie just around the corner;

Are always open to constructive criticism and feedback; and

Always assume they have more to learn about their demanding and difficult profession.

That is why we all want to work for them.

About The Author

Terry Joseph Busch, Ph. D has over forty years of broad professional experience as a teacher, international affairs analyst, manager, senior executive, consultant, and public speaker. His early work experience included stints as an Army Medical Services Corps Officer in Germany and Vietnam, and an Assistant Professorship in the Political Science Department at Denison University in Ohio. His distinguished career with the Central Intelligence Agency included senior assignments as Director of Leadership Analysis in the Directorate of Intelligence, Deputy Inspector General, and Director Human Resource Management. He is now President and CEO of his own management consulting practice.